U.S. Government

Supreme Court

Simon Rose

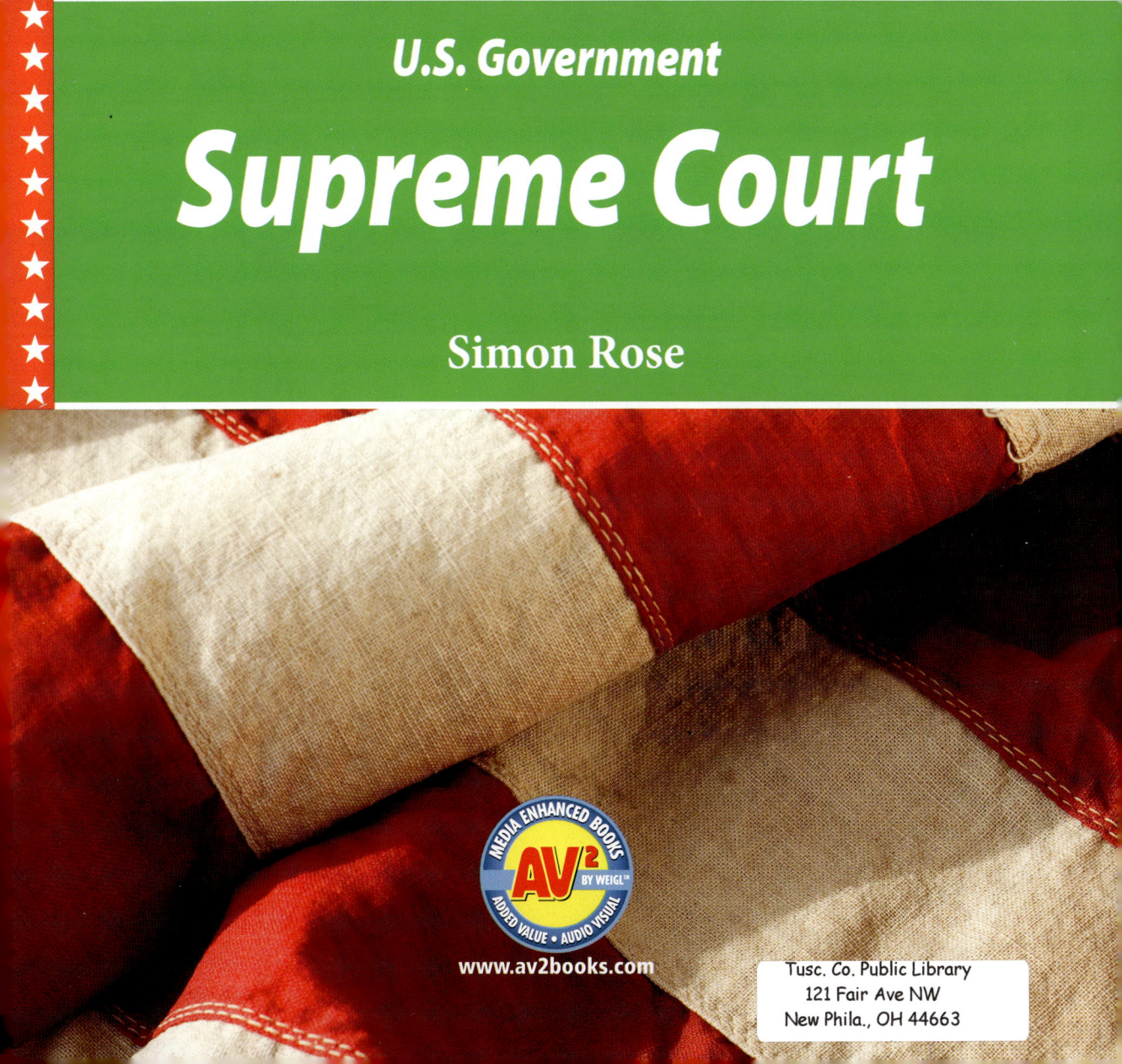

3 1342 00601 8567

AV² provides supplemental features that supplements and complements this book. Weigl's AV² books strive to create inspired learning and engage young minds in a total learning experience.

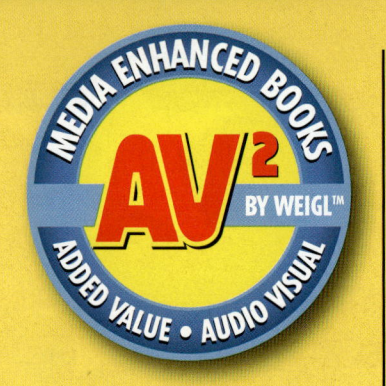

Your AV² Media Enhanced books come alive with...

Audio
Listen to sections of the book read aloud.

Key Words
Study vocabulary, and complete a matching word activity.

Video
Watch informative video clips.

Quizzes
Test your knowledge.

Embedded Weblinks
Gain additional information for research.

Slide Show
View images and captions, and prepare a presentation.

Try This!
Complete activities and hands-on experiments.

... and much, much more!

Go to www.av2books.com, and enter this book's unique code.

BOOK CODE

T225983

AV² by Weigl brings you media enhanced books that support active learning.

Published by AV² by Weigl
350 5th Avenue, 59th Floor
New York, NY 10118

Websites: www.av2books.com   www.weigl.com

Copyright ©2015 AV² by Weigl
All rights reserved. No part of this publication may be reproduced, stored in a retrieval system, or transmitted in any form or by any means, electronic, mechanical, photocopying, recording, or otherwise, without the prior written permission of the publisher.

Library of Congress Cataloging-in-Publication Data

Rose, Simon, 1961- author.
Supreme Court / Simon Rose.
    p. cm. — (U.S. government)
Includes index.
ISBN 978-1-4896-1946-4 (hardcover: alk. paper) — ISBN 978-1-4896-1947-1 (softcover: alk. paper) —
ISBN 978-1-4896-1948-8 (single user ebook) — ISBN 978-1-4896-1949-5 (multi user ebook)
1. United States. Supreme Court. I. Title.
KF8742.R67 2014
347.73'26—dc23
                        2014009522

Printed in the United States of America in North Mankato, Minnesota
1 2 3 4 5 6 7 8 9 0 18 17 16 15 14

052014
WEP270514

Senior Editor: Heather Kissock
Art Director: Terry Paulhus

Weigl acknowledges Getty Images as its primary image supplier for this title.

Every reasonable effort has been made to trace ownership and to obtain permission to reprint copyright material. The publishers would be pleased to have any errors or omissions brought to their attention so that they may be corrected in subsequent printings.

U.S. Government

Contents

AV² Book Code. 2

The Government of the United States . 4

The Federal System 6

The Supreme Court 8

History of the Supreme Court 10

Role of the Supreme Court 12

How the Court System Works 14

The Supreme Court's Home. 16

Key Positions 18

The Court in Session 20

Important Moments 22

Significant Supreme Court Justices. . .24

Issues Facing the Supreme Court. . . .26

Activity 28

Know Your Supreme Court 29

Key Words 30

Index 31

Log on to www.av2.com 32

The Government of the United States

If the United States had no government, there would be no armed forces to protect the country. There would be no laws to keep air and water clean, and there would be no system to manage air traffic at airports. Many aspects of people's lives are affected by government decisions, past and present.

The United States is a democracy, which means its leaders are elected by the people. The national government has three branches. The executive branch carries out laws. It includes the president, the **vice president**, the **cabinet** departments, and government agencies. The legislative branch, which passes laws, is made up of Congress. This branch has two chambers, or parts. They are the Senate and the House of Representatives. The judicial branch, which enforces laws, includes the Supreme Court. This is the highest-level legal body in the United States. The judicial branch also includes several other types of courts.

The three branches of government balance each other. For example, although Congress creates laws, the president has the power to **veto** them. The Supreme Court can decide that laws do not agree with the U.S. **Constitution**. The president is elected, but in special cases, Congress has the power to remove a president from office. The president **nominates** judges to the Supreme Court, but the Senate must approve them.

Washington, D.C.
The main center of the U.S. government is in the country's capital, Washington, D.C.

White House
The president lives and works in the White House. Part of the president's staff works there, too.

Capitol Building
The Senate and the House of Representatives meet in the U.S. Capitol.

Supreme Court Building
The Supreme Court decides cases affecting the nation in the Supreme Court Building.

The carvings over the entry to the Supreme Court stand for liberty, order, and power.

Supreme Court

The Federal System

FOCUS

★ National, state, and local governments share power
★ Each level of government has different areas of responsibility
★ The U.S. government deals with issues affecting the whole country
★ State and local governments have the main responsibility for schools, parks, and public transportation

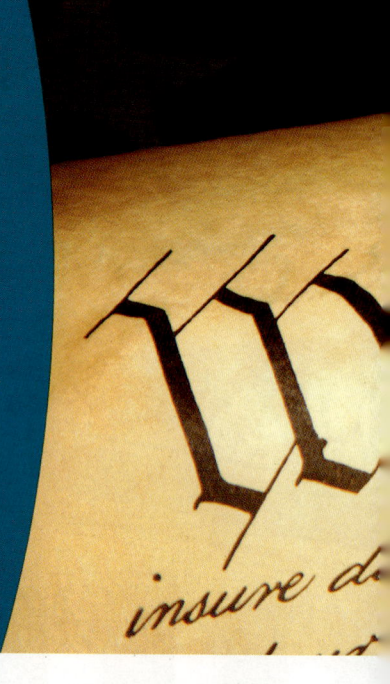

The United States has a federal system of government. This means that power is shared between the national, state, and local governments. The national government is also known as the federal government.

The three levels of government have different powers and responsibilities. Each of the 50 states has its own constitution, and the responsibilities of the federal and state governments are usually clearly defined. However, sometimes disputes occur that have to be settled by the Supreme Court.

The federal government deals with issues affecting the whole country. These include defending the nation, issuing money, and regulating the country's **economy**. The federal government also manages U.S. relations with other nations.

The states have the main responsibility for education, stopping crime, setting up local governments, and regulating businesses within the state. Some responsibilities exist at both the federal and state levels. These include **taxation**, setting up courts, and building highways.

Most local governments have their own fire departments.

There are several types of local governments, including cities, towns, and counties. Counties are known as parishes in Louisiana and boroughs in Alaska. Local governments are responsible for police and emergency medical services. They also manage parks, public transportation, trash collection, and sewer systems.

The Federal Government

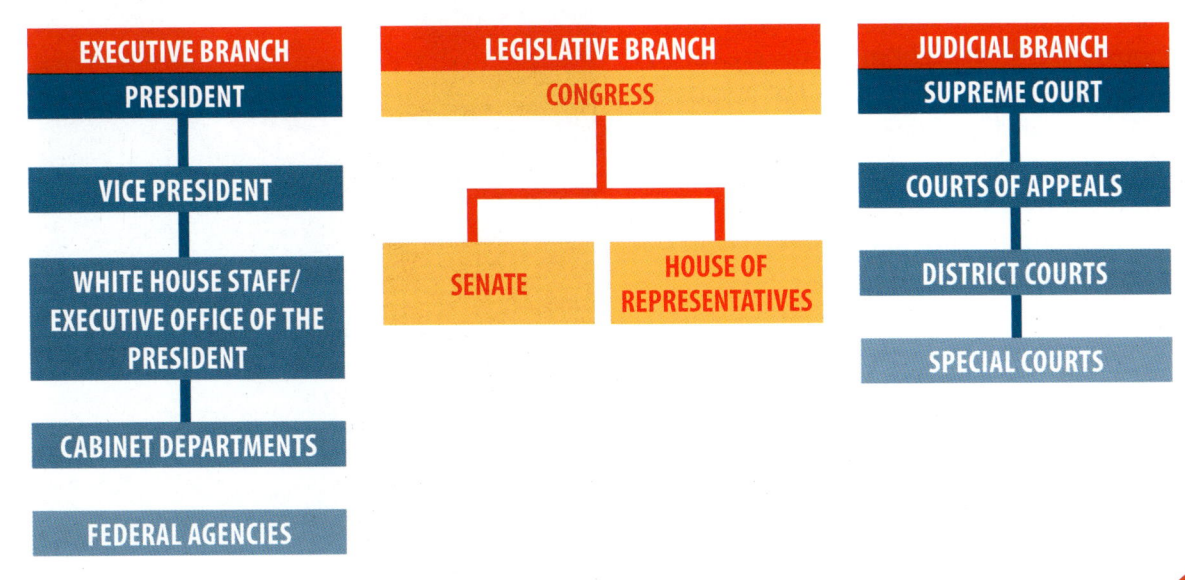

EXECUTIVE BRANCH
- PRESIDENT
- VICE PRESIDENT
- WHITE HOUSE STAFF/ EXECUTIVE OFFICE OF THE PRESIDENT
- CABINET DEPARTMENTS
- FEDERAL AGENCIES

LEGISLATIVE BRANCH
- CONGRESS
  - SENATE
  - HOUSE OF REPRESENTATIVES

JUDICIAL BRANCH
- SUPREME COURT
- COURTS OF APPEALS
- DISTRICT COURTS
- SPECIAL COURTS

Supreme Court

The Supreme Court

FOCUS
- The Supreme Court is the country's highest legal authority
- Judges can remain on the Court for life
- Decisions by the Supreme Court are final

The Supreme Court is the most important court in the United States. Supreme Court judges are called justices. When the justices make a decision in a court case, their ruling becomes the law for the whole country.

The Supreme Court has nine members. The chief justice manages the work of the Court. The other eight members are called associate justices. The number of justices is not set in the U.S. Constitution and can be changed by Congress. Once a judge joins the Supreme Court, he or she can serve for an unlimited amount of time. Justices never have to run for election to the Court. This helps make sure that their decisions are fair and not based on what might be popular with voters.

Antonin Scalia started serving as a Supreme Court justice in 1986.

Most cases that the Supreme Court hears, or considers, are **appeals** of decisions made by lower-level courts. These may be other federal courts or the highest courts in individual states. Often, the Supreme Court justices can choose whether to hear a case or not. If they do so, they can either agree or disagree with the ruling of the lower court. If they choose not to hear a case, the lower-court ruling remains in effect.

When the Supreme Court makes an important ruling, such as its 2012 decision about a major health-care law, journalists often rush out of the building to report the news.

For the Supreme Court to decide a case, a majority of at least five justices must agree on the Court's ruling. A written document called the majority opinion explains the Court's reasons for its decision. Supreme Court decisions are final. They cannot be appealed to another authority.

Supreme Court 9

History of the Supreme Court

FOCUS
- The role of the Supreme Court has changed over time
- The justices have made major decisions for more than 200 years
- Supreme Court rulings can affect the course of U.S. history

The U.S. Constitution, which went into effect in 1789, established the Supreme Court. At first, there were five associate justices and one chief justice. In addition to their duties on the Supreme Court, these justices had to **preside** at lower courts around the country. This responsibility was ended after more lower-court judges were appointed.

The role of the Supreme Court is explained in the Constitution. However, later cases and events changed its role somewhat. The Supreme Court's decision in the 1803 case *Marbury* **versus** *Madison* expanded the power of the Court. This was the first decision in which the Supreme Court struck down, or canceled, a law passed by Congress because the Court found the law to be **unconstitutional**. The Marbury ruling established the Court's power of judicial review, or right to decide whether laws agree with the Constitution or not.

In 1790, the Supreme Court began hearing cases in Independence Hall in Philadelphia, Pennsylvania.

In the 19th century, the Court met in several different locations. The number of justices was changed by Congress a few times. There have been nine justices since 1869.

10 U.S. Government

In 1921, former president William Howard Taft was appointed chief justice. At the time, the Court was located in the Capitol Building. Taft persuaded Congress to provide the Supreme Court with its own building. In 1935, the Court moved to its current home in Washington, D.C.

Many ballots in Florida were not clearly marked in the 2000 presidential election.

The Supreme Court has made decisions that have changed the U.S. justice system. These have included rulings about freedom of speech, the rights of people accused of crimes, and equal rights for women and people of all racial and cultural groups. The Court has decided cases where federal law came in conflict with state law. It has also made important decisions on other topics. In 2000, the results of the presidential election between Al Gore and George W. Bush were very close, and vote totals in Florida were under dispute. The Supreme Court ruled that Florida did not have to recount its votes. This decision, in effect, allowed Bush to become president.

CHANGES OVER TIME

1789 – Congress passes the Judiciary Act, which sets out how the federal court system will work.

1891 – The Judicial Act ends the requirement for Supreme Court justices to preside at lower courts.

1967 – Thurgood Marshall becomes the first African American to serve on the Court.

1981 – Sandra Day O'Connor becomes the first woman appointed to the Supreme Court.

Supreme Court 11

Role of the Supreme Court

FOCUS

★ The justices can decide whether actions of federal officials are legal
★ The Court can rule against the president
★ The justices have overturned laws approved by Congress

The Supreme Court can be compared to a referee. It decides when federal officials have acted against the rules. These rules may be federal laws or the U.S. Constitution. The Supreme Court is also the final judge of what statements in the Constitution mean.

The Court acts as a check on the powers of Congress and the president. The justices of the Supreme Court can rule that the president did something that is not allowed under the Constitution. For example, in 1952, President Harry Truman took control of steel factories during the Korean War. Workers had gone on strike, and Truman claimed that steel was needed to make weapons for the armed forces. However, the Supreme Court ruled that the Constitution does not give the president power to take over industries. Truman had to give up control of the factories.

The Court has struck down laws passed by Congress a number of times. For example, in the 1990s, it canceled a law allowing the president to veto only part of a bill. The Court decided that Congress could not change the rules in the Constitution about vetoes. The Court can also strike down state laws or parts of state constitutions that it decides do not agree with the U.S. Constitution.

In the early 1950s, members of the steelworkers' union voted to strike for higher wages.

SUPREME COURT CASES

The Supreme Court receives about 7,500 requests every year to review cases. However, the justices usually decide to review only about 150 of these. The Court often chooses cases where a decision is needed to make clear what a law means. Sometimes, two or more lower federal courts make different rulings about the same issue. In this situation, the Supreme Court needs to decide the meaning of the law for the whole country.

Supreme Court

How the Court System Works

Federal courts hear cases involving federal laws and the U.S. Constitution. There are two main types of cases. Civil cases settle disagreements between people or between a person and the government. Criminal cases in federal courts involve crimes against U.S. law.

1 The Accused

A criminal case begins when someone is arrested for a crime. The accused person then appears before a judge. The person is officially charged with the crime, and he or she can plead not guilty, or deny having broken the law.

2 Legal Rights

Under the terms of the U.S. Constitution, every person has the right to a fair trial in which a jury decides whether the accused is guilty. A person cannot to be tried twice for the same crime, and people convicted of crimes are protected from cruel punishments.

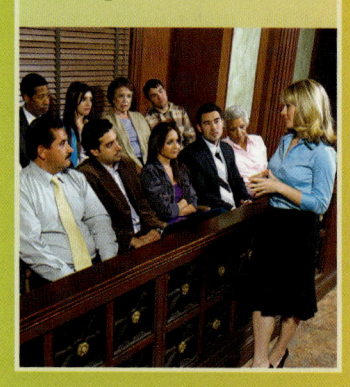

3 Preparing the Case

Before a criminal trial begins, the **prosecution** prepares its case to try to prove that the accused person, or defendant, is guilty. People are considered to be innocent of a crime until they are proven guilty. The defendant and his or her lawyer have time to study the prosecution's evidence and prepare a **defense**.

14 U.S. Government

In most trials, the prosecution and defense lawyers, as well as the defendant, sit at tables facing the judge.

Most arrested people are accused of breaking state laws. More criminal trials are held in state courts than federal courts. However, the legal process is similar.

4 The Trial

Federal criminal trials usually take place in a district court. During the trial, the prosecution and defense lawyers question witnesses and present their arguments. The judge makes decisions such as whether a certain witness should be heard. At the end of the trial, the jury decides whether the defendant is guilty.

5 Appeals

If a person is found guilty, or convicted, he or she can ask a federal court of appeals to review the case. This court looks at the way the trial was conducted and decisions made by the judge. If the appeals court decides the trial was not fair, the accused person may be freed. If it rules the trial was fair, the guilty verdict is upheld.

6 Supreme Court Review

In some cases, a court of appeals decision to uphold a guilty verdict is reviewed by the Supreme Court. This tends to happen when the case involves an important legal question. If the convicted person claims that the way the trial was conducted went against the Constitution, the Supreme Court may choose to hear the case.

Supreme Court 15

The Supreme Court's Home

The Supreme Court Building is located at One First Street, NE, in Washington, D.C. The building was designed by architect Cass Gilbert, who wanted it to look like an ancient Roman temple. Gilbert also tried to make the style of the building similar to the nearby Capitol and Library of Congress.

The Court Chamber
Inside the Supreme Court Building, the justices hear cases in the Court Chamber. This large room, in the shape of a rectangle, has a ceiling that is 44 feet (13 meters) high. The walls and floor are made of marble. Carvings near the ceiling show legal experts of the past. Maroon curtains and marble columns line the wall behind the bench where the justices sit. The curtains hide the door to the justices' Robing Room.

16 U.S. Government

① The Justices' Bench

When the Court is in session, the justices sit behind a long wooden table called the bench. The chief justice sits in the center, with four associate justices on either side. Other Court officials sit nearby. The clerk of the Court works at a desk to the left of the bench. The marshal of the Court calls the Court to order from the right side of the bench.

② Robing Room

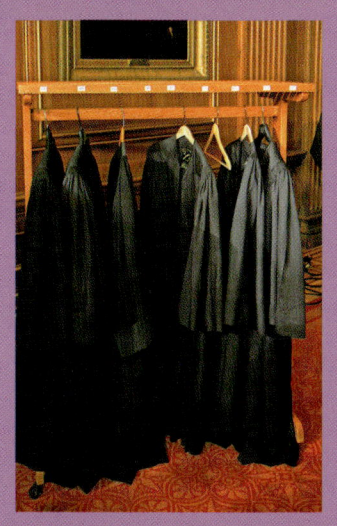

The justices use the Robing Room to put on the special clothing they wear when hearing cases. A large closet is divided into smaller cabinets that line the walls of the Robing Room. Each cabinet has a justice's name on it and holds his or her robe. The justices enter the Robing Room about 10 minutes before a case begins. After putting on their robes, the justices shake hands with one another. This action is meant to show their unity as a group, even though they disagree about specific cases.

③ Lawyers' Seating

Lawyers presenting each side of a case sit at tables in front of the justices' bench. When lawyers address the justices, they stand at a lectern in the center. A white light on the lectern tells them when they have five minutes left to speak. A red light lets them know that they should finish talking. After lawyers present their case to the justices, they sometimes speak to reporters in front of the Supreme Court building.

④ Media Seating

Members of the media sit at red benches on the left side of the Court Chamber. Journalists are not allowed to take photographs or make videos during Supreme Court hearings. They are allowed to draw sketches. No recording devices of any kind are allowed in the Court Chamber while a case is being heard.

Supreme Court 17

Key Positions

In addition to the chief justice and associate justices, more than 475 people work in the Supreme Court Building. These include the counselor to the chief justice and the clerk of the Court. Each justice has several law clerks. Often, these are people who have recently graduated from law school. They help the justice with research that is needed for deciding cases.

▶ Chief Justice

The chief justice presides over the Supreme Court and is the head of the judicial branch of the federal government. The chief justice leads the discussion when the justices need to decide a case they have heard. After the justices vote on a case, if the chief justice votes with the majority, he or she writes the majority opinion or decides which associate justice will write it. At presidential **inaugurations**, the chief justice swears in the newly elected president of the United States.

▶ Associate Justices

Associate justices, as well as the chief justice, all have an equal vote when the Supreme Court is deciding a case. Associate justices write some of the Court's majority opinions. Sometimes, a justice who does not agree with the majority vote writes a dissenting opinion. This document explains why the justice thinks the case should have been decided differently.

John Roberts became chief justice in 2005.

18 U.S. Government

▶ **Counselor to the Chief Justice** The counselor serves as the chief justice's assistant. The counselor provides background information on cases before the Court. He or she also helps with the chief justice's duties managing the court system. The counselor keeps up-to-date with proposals for changes in court procedures. He or she also does research for any public statements made by the chief justice.

▶ **Clerk** The clerk handles Supreme Court recordkeeping and scheduling. He or she keeps track of requests to hear appeals, as well as which cases the justices have agreed to consider. The clerk organizes the Court's calendar, which shows when hearings on various cases will take place. The clerk swears in lawyers who have been approved to argue cases before the Supreme Court.

HOW JUDGES ARE APPOINTED

After the president nominates a justice, the Senate usually takes several steps in considering the appointment. First, the Senate Judiciary Committee reviews the person's qualifications for the position. The committee may hold a hearing at which they question the nominee. If the committee votes in favor of approval, the nomination is then considered by the entire Senate. The Senate must approve the nominee by a majority vote before he or she can take office.

In 1987, the Senate voted not to approve President Ronald Reagan's nomination of Robert Bork for associate justice.

Supreme Court

The Court in Session

FOCUS

★ A Court term lasts about nine months
★ When a case is heard, lawyers are allowed 30 minutes each to make their arguments
★ Justices often ask the lawyers questions
★ Proceedings are open to the public

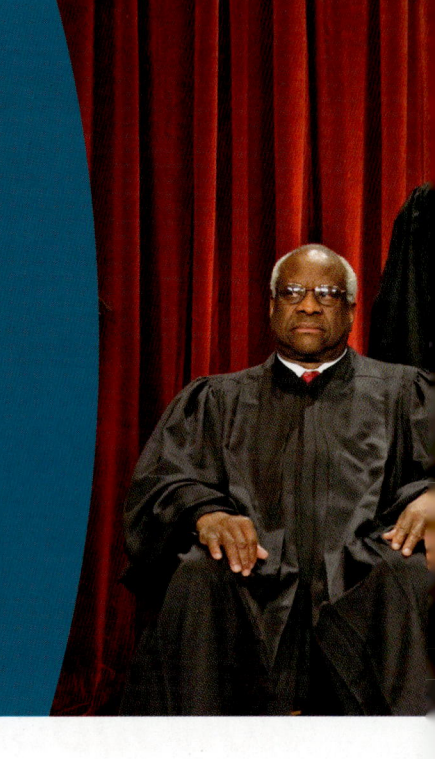

A Supreme Court **term** begins on the first Monday in October. It usually continues until late June of the following year. Each term is divided into sittings and recesses, which last about two weeks each. During sittings, justices hear cases and give their rulings. They consider the business presented to the Court and write their opinions on cases during recesses.

Supreme Court cases usually begin when the losing party in a lower court asks the justices to review and change the decision. In most situations, if four justices agree to hear the case, it is added to the Court's calendar. The lawyers for each side then submit written arguments to the Court.

On the scheduled date, the lawyers go to the Court Chamber to make their oral arguments. Each side has 30 minutes to present its case. The justices also ask questions during this period. Only the lawyers are questioned. No witnesses are called to testify at Supreme Court hearings. Members of the public attend Court hearings but are not allowed to speak.

While justices consider a case inside the Court, protesters outside sometimes try to influence their decision. In the 2000 presidential election case, supporters of candidates Al Gore and George W. Bush rallied outside the Court.

20 U.S. Government

After hearing oral arguments in the Court Chamber, each justice reviews the case with his or her law clerks. The justices then discuss the case among themselves and cast their votes. Supreme Court decisions become part of U.S. law. All decisions carry the same weight, whether they are reached by votes of 5–4, 6–3, 7–2, 8–1, or 9–0. A 9–0 ruling is called a unanimous decision.

The Supreme Court term ends at the beginning of the summer. However, the justices and their staffs continue working. They may do research to prepare for the new term in the fall. They may also be called on to make emergency rulings, such as whether to stop the execution of a person convicted of murder until an appeal can be heard.

Supreme Court decisions are collected on websites for lawyers and others to consult.

ROBES OF OFFICE

The chief justice and associate justices wear plain black robes when the Court is in session. They also wear them for events such presidential inaugurations or when new justices are sworn in as members of the Court. In the Court's early years, the justices' robes had red fronts. However, the color was soon changed to all-black. Justices wear business clothing beneath their robes.

Supreme Court

Important Moments

The Supreme Court has been involved in some of the key moments in American history. Some of its decisions have expanded the rights of individuals. At times, there have been disputes between the Court and the president.

Near v. Minnesota Case 1931

For more than a century, the First Amendment to the U.S. Constitution had protected freedom of the press against actions by the federal government. However, it was not clear until the Supreme Court's *Near v. Minnesota* decision in 1931 that the Constitution also protected press freedom from state actions. In Minnesota, Jay Near's newspaper, the *Saturday Press*, had published stories linking local politicians with criminals. The government of Minnesota ordered the newspaper to shut down. It declared that the *Saturday Press* was publishing harmful material. The Supreme Court ruled that the shutdown violated the Constitution. The decision, written by Chief Justice Charles Evans Hughes, stated that only in rare cases, such as during a wartime emergency, could a state government keep a newspaper from publishing.

President Franklin D. Roosevelt Fights the Supreme Court 1937

During the **Great Depression** of the 1930s, President Franklin D. Roosevelt convinced Congress to pass a number of laws intended to help the economy. However, the Supreme Court struck down some of these laws as unconstitutional. In 1937, Roosevelt asked Congress to add six justices to the Court. Roosevelt hoped that this would allow him to appoint justices who were more likely to approve of his policies. However, many people opposed the president's plan. He was accused of trying to "pack the court" with supporters and interfere with the Court's independence. The president backed down.

22 U.S. Government

| **1931** Near v. Minnesota Case | **1937** President Franklin D. Roosevelt Fights the Supreme Court | **1963** Gideon v. Wainwright Case | **1966** Miranda v. Arizona Case | **1974** United States v. Nixon Case |

Gideon v. Wainwright Case 1963

In 1961, Clarence Earl Gideon was accused of stealing from a Florida pool hall. At his trial, Gideon said he could not afford to hire a lawyer. The state refused to provide one for him. Gideon was convicted and sentenced to prison. From there, he wrote to the Supreme Court. He claimed that the Sixth Amendment gave everyone the right to a lawyer. The Supreme Court agreed. The *Gideon v. Wainwright* case established the legal right that courts must provide lawyers for poor people accused of crimes. At his second trial, helped by a lawyer, Gideon won his freedom.

Miranda v. Arizona Case 1966

Ernesto Miranda was identified by a crime victim and arrested. When police officers questioned him, Miranda was not informed of his basic rights as written in the Constitution. Under the Fifth Amendment, Miranda had the right to not **incriminate** himself. Miranda confessed to the crime. However, his lawyer argued that this evidence should not be allowed at the trial. The Supreme Court agreed. As a result of the *Miranda v. Arizona* case, the police are required to tell accused people, as soon as they are arrested, that they have the right to remain silent.

United States v. Nixon Case 1974

During the **Watergate scandal**, it was discovered that President Richard Nixon had made tape recordings of his conversations in the White House. Prosecutors investigating the scandal believed the tapes could provide important evidence. Nixon claimed that the **executive privilege** he had as president allowed him to keep the tapes private. However, in *United States v. Nixon*, the Supreme Court ruled that the president is not above the legal process. Nixon was ordered to release the tapes. In August 1974, he became the first president to resign from office.

Supreme Court

Significant Supreme Court Justices

Many people have served on the Supreme Court since it was first established. Some justices held other important positions before joining the Court. For many years, all justices were white and male. In recent decades, the Court's membership has become more diverse.

John Jay (in office 1789–1795)

John Jay (1745–1829) was the first chief justice of the United States. During the American Revolution, he convinced Spain to loan money to the United States to help pay for the war. Jay also helped negotiate the 1783 Treaty of Paris, in which Great Britain agreed to American independence. As chief justice, Jay established many of the rules and procedures of the Supreme Court. He later served as the governor of New York. In 1800, President John Adams offered to make him chief justice again, but Jay declined.

John Marshall (in office 1801–1835)

John Marshall (1755–1835) served as chief justice of the Supreme Court longer than any other justice to date. He held the office for 34 years. Marshall fought in the American Revolution and served in the Virginia legislature. He was also secretary of state under President John Adams. During his time as chief justice, Marshall established the Supreme Court as the final authority on the meaning of the U.S. Constitution.

U.S. Government

Oliver Wendell Holmes, Jr. (in office 1902–1932)

Oliver Wendell Holmes, Jr. (1841–1935), was known for making strong legal arguments in his decisions. Holmes believed that legislatures should make laws that represented the people's will, and he was not eager to strike down laws passed by Congress or the states. He also strongly supported the right of free speech. In his majority opinion in the 1919 case *Schenck v. United States*, he stated that a government could limit freedom of speech only if there was a "clear and present danger" that the speech would harm the country.

Thurgood Marshall (in office 1967–1991)

Thurgood Marshall (1908–1993) worked for equal rights for African Americans. As a lawyer, he argued the *Brown v. Board of Education* case in front of the Supreme Court. He urged the Court to rule that segregated school systems, in which black children were forced to attend separate schools from white students, violated the Constitution. His argument was successful. In 1954, the Supreme Court issued a unanimous decision against segregated schools. After joining the Court, Marshall continued to be a strong supporter of **civil liberties**.

Sandra Day O'Connor (in office 1981–2006)

Sandra Day O'Connor (born 1930) worked as a lawyer and was also elected for two terms to the Arizona Senate. She served as the state senate's majority leader, the first woman in the United States to hold such a position. She was a judge on the Arizona court of appeals before President Ronald Reagan nominated her to the U.S. Supreme Court in 1981. On the Court, she was known as a moderate who helped the justices come together to make a decision. O'Connor retired in 2006 after serving on the Supreme Court for 24 years.

Issues Facing the Supreme Court

FOCUS

★ *Affirmative action, especially in college admissions*
★ *Possible regulation of the internet*
★ *Court decisions and political considerations*

The Supreme Court deals with difficult issues such as affirmative action and laws about new technologies. It also faces questions about the independence of judges. African Americans, women, Hispanic Americans, and other cultural groups have faced discrimination, or unfair treatment, in the United States. Affirmative action refers to policies intended to make up for this discrimination. For example, some colleges consider a student's race or cultural group, as well as whether the student is male or female, as one factor among many others when deciding whether to admit that student.

Some people think affirmative action is needed because certain groups have not had equal access to quality education in the past. Other people believe affirmative action is itself a form of discrimination. Since the 1970s, the Supreme Court has decided several affirmative action cases. It has tried to set up rules about which policies are or are not legal.

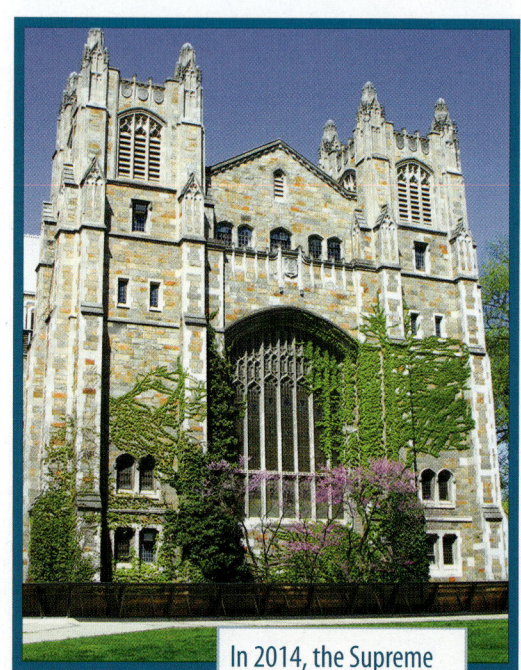

In 2014, the Supreme Court decided an affirmative action case affecting the University of Michigan and other colleges in that state.

U.S. Government

The growth of the internet has created new legal issues. Government officials may force internet sites to shut down or make it illegal for children to visit some sites because officials believe they are harmful. Some people think such actions are needed. Others feel that they violate the right to freedom of speech. Companies may collect information about people using the internet. Many companies believe such practices are a normal part of doing business. A number of people think that the right to privacy of internet users needs to be better protected. Some of these legal questions have already reached the Supreme Court. Others will in the future.

Clarence Thomas, appointed by Republican President George H. W. Bush, and Ruth Bader Ginsburg, named by Democratic President Bill Clinton, often vote on opposite sides in Supreme Court decisions.

Supreme Court justices are expected to make decisions based on the law and not political considerations. In recent years, some people have said the Court has become too political. Presidents from both major political parties, Republicans and Democrats, often appoint justices who tend to agree with their views. Some people think there are, in effect, Republican and Democratic justices. The justices say that this is not true and that decisions are not based on politics. If Americans do not believe Supreme Court rulings are fair, people may not trust and respect Court decisions.

Activity

What is a debate?

When people **debate** a topic, two sides take a different viewpoint about one idea. They present logical arguments to support their views. Usually, each person or team is given a set amount of time to present its case. The presenters take turns stating their arguments until the total time set aside for the debate is used up. Sometimes, there is an audience in the room listening to the presentations. Later, the members of the audience vote for the person or team they think made the most persuasive arguments.

Debating is an important skill. It helps people to think about ideas carefully. It also helps them develop ways of speaking that others can follow easily. Some schools have organized debating clubs as part of their after-school activities. Schools often hold debates in their history class or as part of studying about world events.

Debate this!

Every day, the news is filled with the issues facing the United States and its citizens. These issues are debated within the federal government and by Americans around the country. People often have different views of these issues and support different solutions. Here is an issue that has been discussed across the country. Gather your friends or classmates, and divide into two teams to debate the issue. Each team should take time to research the issue and develop solid arguments for its side.

In 1976, the Supreme Court upheld a federal law that limits the amount of money a person can contribute, or give, to the political **campaign** of one candidate. Since then, the Court has struck down other laws limiting how much a person could give in total to candidates or how much a company could spend to affect the outcome of an election.

Some people believe that individuals and companies should be able to spend their money without restrictions. They think that controlling contributions amounts to limiting free speech. Others believe limiting contributions keeps elections fair for all candidates. Limits may also keep large contributors from receiving special treatment from politicians.

? Should the Supreme Court limit campaign contributions?

★ Know Your Supreme Court

1 Since what year has the Supreme Court had nine justices?

2 Which former president became chief justice in 1921?

3 About how many requests to review cases does the Supreme Court receive every year?

4 In what year was the *Marbury v. Madison* case decided?

5 On what day does each Supreme Court term begin?

6 Who was the first female Supreme Court justice?

7 In what decision did the Supreme Court strike down segregated schools?

8 When did the Supreme Court move into its current building?

9 At least how many justices must agree on a Supreme Court ruling?

10 Who was the longest-serving chief justice of the Supreme Court?

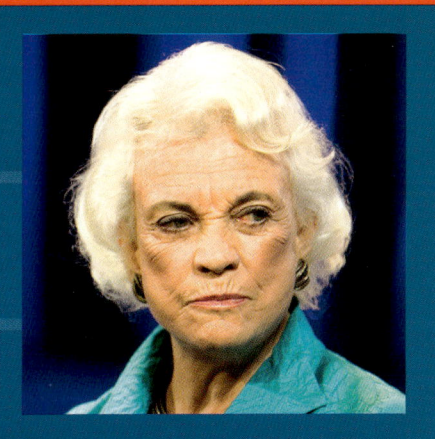

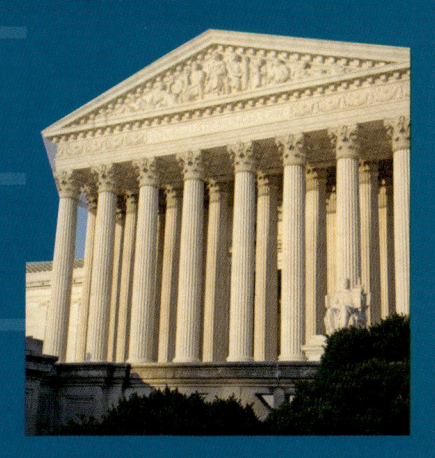

ANSWER KEY

1 1869 **2** William Howard Taft **3** 7,500 **4** 1803 **5** The first Monday in October **6** Sandra Day O'Connor **7** *Brown v. Board of Education* **8** 1935 **9** Five **10** John Marshall

Supreme Court 29

Key Words

appeals: requests to a higher court to review decisions of lower courts and decide whether they were fair and correct

cabinet: a group of people, many of them the heads of government departments, who give advice to the president

campaign: a series of activities to achieve a particular purpose, such as being elected to office

civil liberties: basic rights of all citizens in a democracy, such as freedom of speech and from arrest without showing cause

constitution: a document that defines and limits the powers of a government and describes how that government is organized

defense: evidence and arguments to show that someone accused of a crime is not guilty

economy: the system by which a country's goods and services are produced, bought, and sold

executive privilege: the president's right to keep some information private to protect the nation

Great Depression: a time of harsh economic conditions during the 1930s when some banks closed and many people lost their homes, farms, and jobs

inaugurations: ceremonies where newly elected officials are sworn into public office

incriminate: to make oneself seem guilty of something

nominates: names to fill an official position or chooses a candidate for office

preside: to be in charge of

prosecution: the lawyers trying to prove the guilt of a person accused of a crime

taxation: the process by which a government raises money from its citizens or residents to pay for the services it provides

term: the length of time for which the Supreme Court meets regularly to hear and decide cases

unconstitutional: against the terms of the United States Constitution

versus: against, often shortened to *v.*

veto: a power used by the president to stop a bill from becoming law

vice president: the person who holds the rank just below the president of the United States

Watergate scandal: a series of crimes and improper actions involving President Richard Nixon and officials working for him

Index

affirmative action 26
African Americans 11, 25, 26
appeals 7, 9, 15, 19, 21, 25
associate justices 8, 10, 17, 18, 19, 21

Bush, George W. 11, 20, 27

campaign contributions 28
chief justices 8, 10, 11, 17, 18, 19, 21, 22, 24, 29
clerk of the Court 17, 18, 19
Congress 4, 7, 8, 10, 11, 12, 13, 16, 22, 25
constitutions 4, 6, 8, 10, 12, 13, 14, 15, 22, 23, 24, 25,
counselor to chief justice 18, 19
criminal cases 14, 15

defense 14, 15
district courts 7, 15

federal courts 9, 11, 13, 14, 15
free speech 11, 25, 27, 28

Gilbert, Cass 16
Gore, Al 11, 20
Great Depression 22

Holmes, Oliver Wendell, Jr. 25

inaugurations 18, 21
internet 26, 27

Jay, John 24

lawyers 14, 15, 17, 19, 20, 21, 23, 25

Marshall, John 24, 29
Marshall, Thurgood 11, 25

Nixon, Richard 23
nominating 4, 19, 25

O'Connor, Sandra Day 11, 25, 29

privacy 27
prosecution 14, 15, 23

Reagan, Ronald 19, 25
Roberts, John 18
robes 17, 21
Roosevelt, Franklin D. 22, 23
rulings and decisions 8, 9, 10, 11, 13, 15, 20, 21, 22, 25, 26, 27, 29

Scalia, Antonin 8
Senate 4, 5, 7, 19, 25
state courts 15
Supreme Court building 5, 9, 11, 16, 17, 18, 29

Taft, William Howard 11, 29
terms 20, 21, 25, 29
Truman, Harry 12

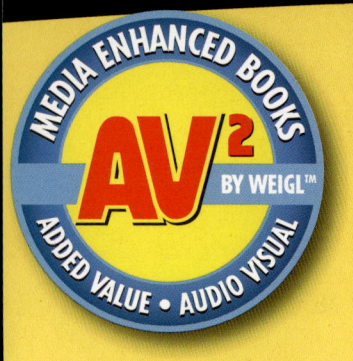

Log on to www.av2books.com

AV² by Weigl brings you media enhanced books that support active learning. Go to www.av2books.com, and enter the special code found on page 2 of this book. You will gain access to enriched and enhanced content that supplements and complements this book. Content includes video, audio, weblinks, quizzes, a slide show, and activities.

AV² Online Navigation

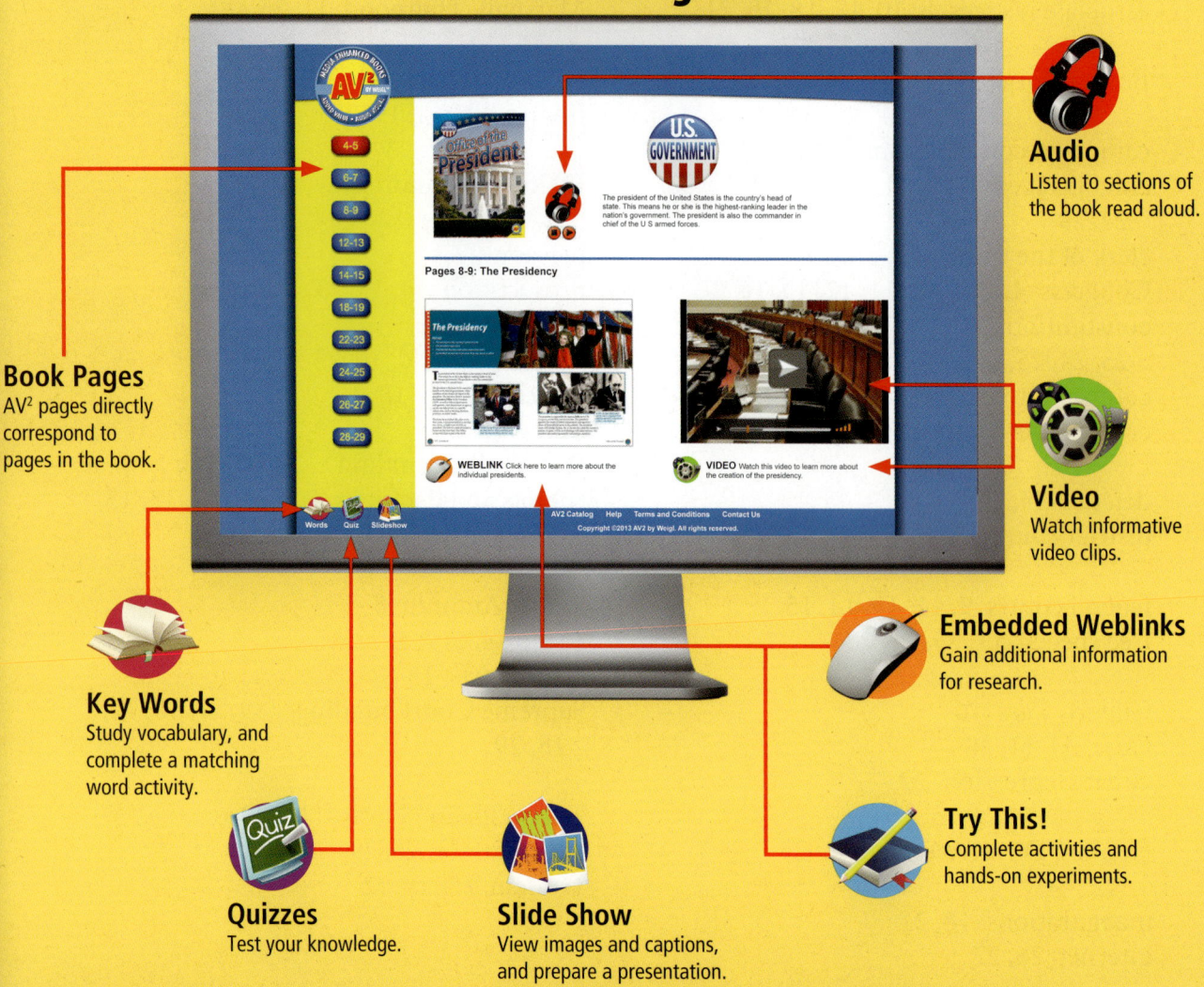

Audio
Listen to sections of the book read aloud.

Video
Watch informative video clips.

Embedded Weblinks
Gain additional information for research.

Try This!
Complete activities and hands-on experiments.

Book Pages
AV² pages directly correspond to pages in the book.

Key Words
Study vocabulary, and complete a matching word activity.

Quizzes
Test your knowledge.

Slide Show
View images and captions, and prepare a presentation.

AV² was built to bridge the gap between print and digital. We encourage you to tell us what you like and what you want to see in the future.

Sign up to be an AV² Ambassador at www.av2books.com/ambassador.

Due to the dynamic nature of the Internet, some of the URLs and activities provided as part of AV² by Weigl may have changed or ceased to exist. AV² by Weigl accepts no responsibility for any such changes. All media enhanced books are regularly monitored to update addresses and sites in a timely manner. Contact AV² by Weigl at 1-866-649-3445 or av2books@weigl.com with any questions, comments, or feedback.